MARBLE PAINTING

Project Book

Learn how to create marble
rock painting decor for
your home

5 projects inside

O2

Welcome to the world of Marble painting

This kit has been specifically designed for adults only.

Marble Painting is a fun, easy and quick skill to learn – all you need is a couple of colours of paint, the object you would like to showcase your individual marbling creation on and lastly your imagination!

You can marble almost ANYTHING! It's a lovely way to combine all of your favourite colours in one place, let them blend together in whichever way they decide to move, and see what beautiful piece of abstract art you are left with. The best bit about it is that every single piece you make will be distinctive and unique to only you! It's also a very therapeutic skill, looking on as your colours all tilt and roll into one – there's something quite relaxing about that isn't there!? What's more, once you have finished your fantastic masterpiece, you can either keep it for yourself as a keepsake or wrap it up and give a beautiful handmade gift to someone you love!

Most marbling techniques involve only a few colours initially, but the beauty of it is you can use different tools to add extra design and uniqueness to your creation, maybe you'd like to try feathering your marbling using a toothpick? (we will get into that a little later on!) Or by using an old skewer, maybe a plastic fork to drag lines through the paint? The list really is endless, let your imagination go wild and experiment with your paint! So, shall we get marbling?!

Top Tips - Before starting any craft involving paint, always cover your work surface with an easy to wipe mat/tablecloth or alternatively, a couple of bits of old newspaper will do the trick!

KIT CONTENTS

WHAT'S INCLUDED:
· 6 x smooth pebbles
· Acrylic Paint
· Wooden Stirrer

WHAT YOU'LL NEED

· Toothpick/skewers/needle
· Pouring Medium/ water
· Disposable Gloves
· A paint palette or little pots to mix your paint colours
· A small paintbrush
· Paper plate or drying rack

Ingredients:
Acrylic resin emulsion, Calcium carbonate, Glycerin, 2-Hydroxyethyl cellulose, Triethanolamine, Methyl 4-hydroxybenzoate, Hydroxyethyl cellulose, Water. Pigment Blue,phloxine and permanent violet

THE BASICS

When marbling your first piece of work, you will need a couple of different colours of paint, 2-3 colours works well, but obviously the more colourful and different you would like your piece of art to look the more colours you can add throughout! You also don't have to start with all the colours you intend to use, you may find as you go through your marbling process that you want to add another colour into the mix — and that's okay!

Acrylic paint is a good medium to start with for marbling, this is because it is one of the most versatile paints you can use. For best results, always marble on an object with a smooth surface! This will really enable your paint to move freely around your work and enhance the end product. For example, a pebble works well for marbling as you have a lovely surface to cover, but the slightly curved edges are great when it comes to the tilting technique.

To help your acrylic paint really flow effortlessly, you can add a tiny bit of water to loosen up the consistency. You can do this to each individual colour by popping a little bit of your paint into a palette or little cups/paint pots and then add the water and give it a good mix with a wooden stirrer. Alternatively, if you have any pouring medium at home — this also works brilliantly to help improve the consistency of the paint allowing them to pour more fluidly.

WARNINGS!

All the makes included in this book are designed specifically for adults.

Keep all ingredients and finished products out of the reach of children.

Some ingredients may irritate; always avoid contact with skin and eyes. If ingredients come into contact with eyes or skin, wash with cold water immediately.

Do not ingest; if accidentally ingested drink water and seek medical advice.

We recommend wearing old clothes or overalls when partaking in creative activities. Cover work surfaces to avoid mess.

TIPS

The art of marbling is quite simple really, all you will be doing is transferring your paint onto the surface you have chosen, and then it's up to you how you decide to move the paint to create different marbling effects. There are three main techniques you could try:

Tilting

Drip 1-2 (don't be scared to try more!) drops of paint onto your smooth surface area.
This effect is created by carefully tilting your pebble in different directions allowing the paint to marble together. Keep tilting until you are happy with what you see!

Swirling

Drip 2-3 (add an extra color this time!) drops of paint onto your smooth surface area. Carefully tilt again but not too much this time, just enough to cover the whole surface.
Run your toothpick up and down your surface (even side to side if you like) to create some beautiful swirled effects.

Dipped

Drip 2-3 colours of paint onto a flat surface area, a paper plate or a piece of paper works great for this. Now carefully dip your object into the paint being careful not to move it around too much! Let it sit for less than a minute and then very gently lift it up to reveal your dipped marbling effect.

Top Tip – After trying the tilting and swirling method, you will find you will have lots of excess paint that has dripped from your pebble onto your paper which has subsequently created its own marbling affect. Use this excess paint to try the dipped/rolling method to create an even more unique design!

MAKE WITH KIT CONTENTS!

MARBLE ROCK

MARBLE ROCK

This booklet will take you step by step through this beautiful marble painting process, as well as four more designs!

YOU WILL NEED

- Toothpick
- Plastic Spoon
- Gloves
- Little pots

KIT CONTAINS

- 6 x Smooth Pebbles
- Acrylic Paint
- Wooden Stirrer

METHOD

1. Get your paint, little pots and pebbles ready. Pop your gloves on and make sure to cover the work surface before you start!

2. One by one, drip your colours onto your pebble. You want to drip enough paint so that your colours reach the end of your pebble but not too much that one colour overtakes another. The easiest way to do this would be in lines.

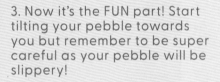

3. Now it's the FUN part! Start tilting your pebble towards you but remember to be super careful as your pebble will be slippery!

4. Once you have held your pebble up for a few minutes, grab your toothpick and start running through the paint in slow movements up and down until you have reached the end of your pebble.

5. Add a bit more paint to your pebble, covering the whole surface. You could even experiment and create little puddle drops with a plastic spoon or a pipette if you have one!

6. Once your whole pebble is covered, get running your toothpick through the paint again, this time you could try side to side! Once you're happy with your colours lay your pebble flat on a drying rack or on a paper plate and let it dry for 24-48hrs.

NOTES

Use the space below to make your own personal notes on the previous project to help when you come back to make it again!

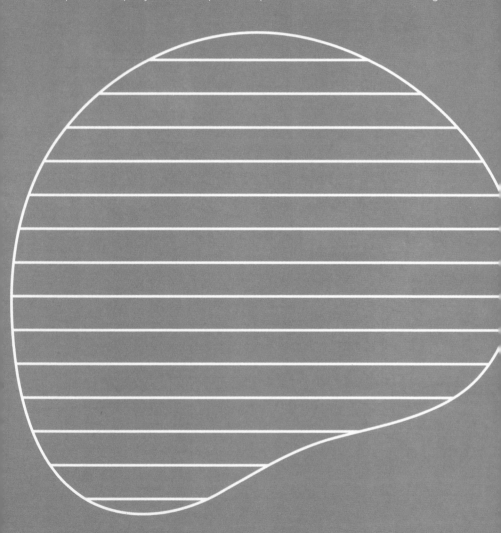

HEXAGON COASTER

HEXAGON COASTER

Bring some colour to your life (and your room) with these bold drinks coasters! Choose the colours that suit you and make a statement!

YOU WILL NEED

· Coaster
· Acrylic Paint
· Wooden Stirrer
· Gloves
· Water/ Marbling medium
· Plastic pots/ Mixing palette

METHOD

1. Choose 2-3 colours of paint and pop them in your mixing palette/plastic cups. Mix a very small amount of water OR marbling medium if you have it and mix with a wooden stirrer. Elevate your coaster on a paper cup in preparation to enable the paint to drip off easier and prevent your coaster from sticking to your surface.

2. Starting with one colour at a time, use a plastic spoon to gently drip your paint in dollops onto your coaster.

3. Keep repeating this process until you have used up all your paint!

4. Start tilting!

5. Very slowly, keep tilting your coaster in different directions until all of the surface area is covered and you are happy with your design.

6. Once finished, leave your coaster to dry on top of your paper cup for 24-48hrs. Once dry you can touch up the edges with some of your leftover white paint and a small paintbrush!

NOTES

Use the space below to make your own personal notes on the previous project to help when you come back to make it again!

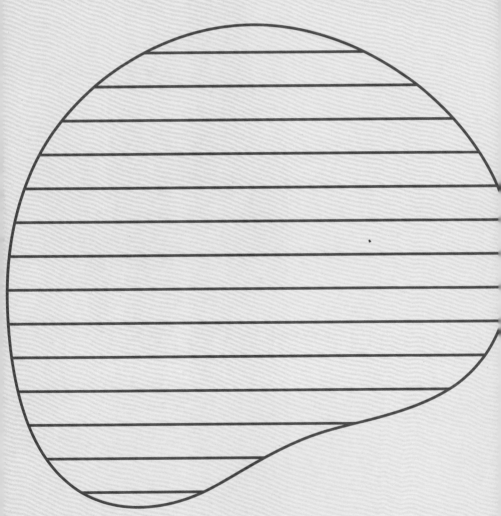

HEART HANGING

HEART HANGING

Express some love with this cute heart hanging. Show yourself some love or give as a gift to a friend or loved one!

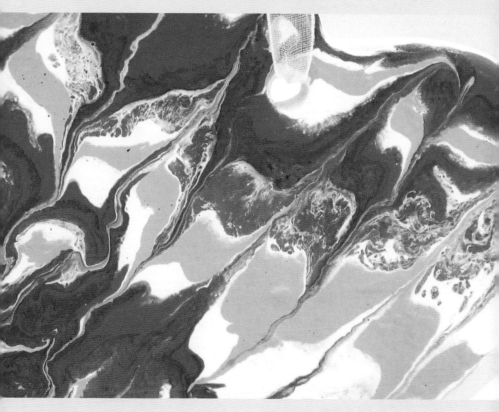

YOU WILL NEED

- Heart wall hanging
- Acrylic Paint
- Wooden Stirrer
- Gloves
- Mixing palette/ Plastic pots

METHOD

1. Put 3-4 colours of paint in your palette and, as you did before, add a little of your water or marbling medium to each of your colours (1 part paint to 1 part medium). If your decoration has a ribbon or thread attached to it, please remove this first before marbling.

2. Using your plastic spoon, slowly drag across your heart, enabling the paint to drip in lines horizontally. Start to create a rhythm in which you would like your colours to be shown.

3. Once you have your formation, continue dripping each colour until the whole of your decoration is covered.

4. Wait a few minutes, and watch as your colours slowly start to merge and naturally marble into one another!

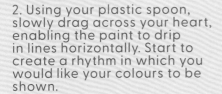

5. Drag your toothpick through the layers of paint up and down or side to side to reveal a beautiful swirled affect.

6. Once you have done your whole heart, leave this laying on the top of the cup for 24-48hrs to dry. Once dry, re-attach your ribbon and you're ready to hang up your decoration!

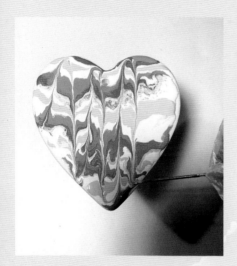

NOTES

Use the space below to make your own personal notes on the previous project to help when you come back to make it again!

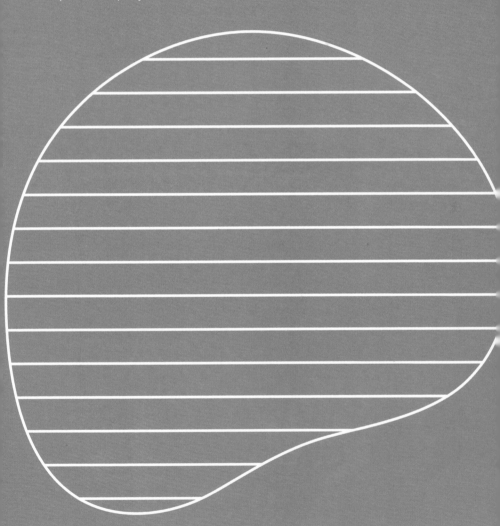

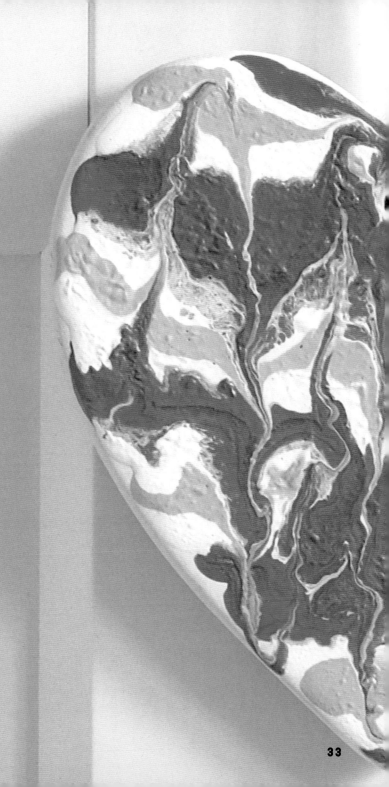

STAR BUNTING

STAR
BUNTING

Using the following steps, you can create this cool and vibrant bunting design with the colours of your choice!

YOU WILL NEED

·Bunting
·Disposible tray
·Wooden Stirrer
·Gloves
·Pouring medium
·Paper cups

METHOD

1. Make sure your work surface is clean and protected, place the disposible tray onto a protected surface.

2. Using the paper cups pour 5ml of each acrylic paint into each cup.

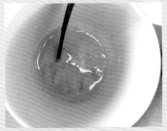

3. Pour 10ml of the pouring medium into each cup and mix each paint until fully mixed, it should be a creamy consistency.

4. Spoon each colour onto the tray (One colour at a time) going in different directions and covering certain areas of the tray. Spoon the paint dripping it across the other colours, creating an abstract mix.

5. Once each colour has been carefully spooned into the tray, use a cocktail stick or lolly pop stick, and gently stroke through the paint in a horizontal direction, forming a line. (Form more lines above), if you've used more than 3 colours make sure you gently move the paint as it mixes to avoid the colours turning brown.

6. Once happy with the marbling effect, dip each star into the best areas of marbling paint and gently lift off the paint, try not to move the star around, left or right, otherwise this will smudge.

7. Once out flip over to air dry. Repeat the process selecting different areas of the paint.

8. Once dry thread your choice of string through each hole to hang and decorate. Perfect for parties and room décor.

NOTES

Use the space below to make your own personal notes on the previous project to help when you come back to make it again!

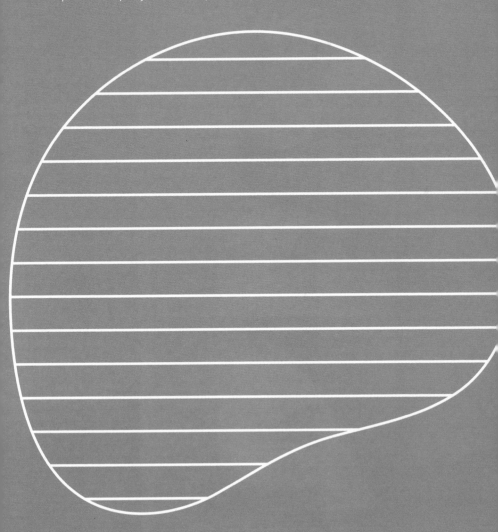

VARNISH VASES

VARNISH VASES

Give your plant pal a new outfit and watch it bloom!

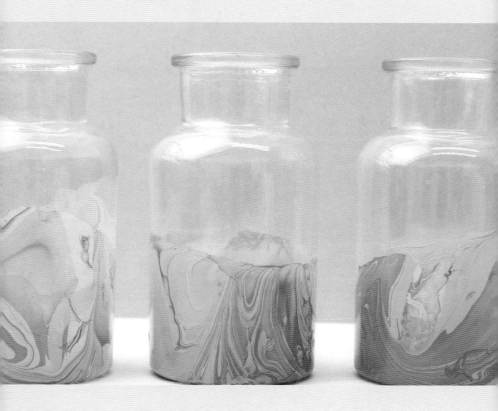

YOU WILL NEED

.Nail Varnish
.Vase/bottle
.Bowl
.Wooden stick
.Cocktail stick

METHOD

1. Make sure your work surface is clean and protected. Using a clean bowl, fill up with water leaving about an inch gap from the top. Make sure you are using the nail varnishes in a well-ventilated space.

2. Have your nail varnishes ready, also think about the colours you are using and whether they compliment each other. In this make we've used some bright summer colours but have only used three colours. To give yourself more time, unscrew the lids so they are ready to be poured.

3. Pouring your first nail varnish into the water. The first colour will disperse quite quickly into the water this will be a good base, so you may need to add more of the colour at the end.

4. Add in the next colour in a circular motion or figure of eight.

5. Add in the next colour, using the same pouring motion.

6. Once you've poured all varnishes into the water, Use a cocktail or wooden stick, and start slowly moving the nail varnishes around in different directions to create a marbling effect. To bring the first colour into the marbling you can move it from the edges of the bowl. Try out different techniques by moving the varnishes, left to right or in a figure of eight. Remember not to do this process too quickly.

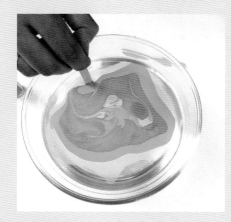

7. Once you're happy with the marbled pattern, get your vase ready and carefully place into the water, submerging the bottom quarter of the vase and slowly lift out. The water should start to run off the glass. Place upside down to dry. Try different techniques by either fully submerging the glass vase or using one side and twist the vase around whilst lifting it out of the water.

NOTES

Use the space below to make your own personal notes on the previous project to help when you come back to make it again!

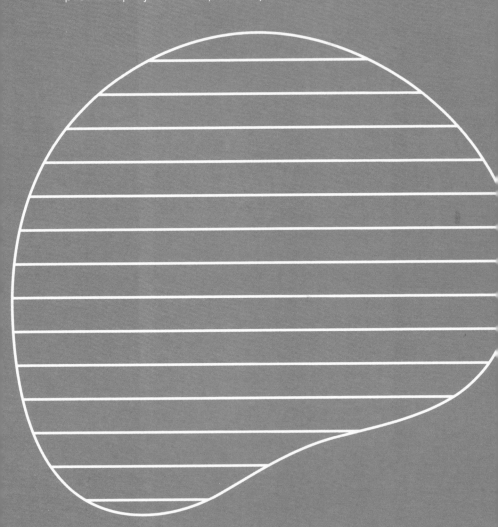

THE CRAFT LAB
MARBLE PAINTING KIT

This homemade marble painting kit includes all the things you need to make your very own marble creations, perfect for a little personal creativity or gifting to a loved one. This kit also includes 4 further designs for you to enjoy. We'll have you marble painting like the pro's! So let's get creative!

⚠ WARNING

- After skin contact: Wash straight away with soap and water.
- After eye contact: Rinse and bathe opened eye with water for 10 minutes.
- After Ingestion: Wash out mouth with water. Consult medical advice.

ISBN 978-1-7396275-0-8

9 781739 627508